INTRODUCTION

In 1969 my first book on walks in Derbyshir
walks of varying lengths. Four years later
ever since. Using that book as a backbone, I
them. I used in the main the same paths, b
the current car-parks and facilities that n

These fifteen walks are among my favourites in the Peak Di...
the tremendous variety of walking countryside there is in such a small area. The
majority of the walks are in the less popular areas which is good, for here you are
away from the masses and enjoying just as interesting and delectable scenery. Some,
through necessity, pass through popular areas, but the routes are challenging and
should provide you with different views of well-known areas.

All the walks are circular from a car park, and I have striven to plan the routes to
include at least one inn either actually on the route or just off it. Whilst I have
endeavoured to make my maps and descriptions as clear as possible, it is always
necessary for you to carry the appropriate Outdoor Leisure map with you to give you
even clearer knowledge of the area you are passing through.

Walking in the Peak District is one of the delights of life, and I hope these walks
give you even more enjoyment from walking in this region of England.

Happy Walking!

John N. Merrill

JOHN N. MERRILL
DERBYSHIRE. 1986

KINDER'S THREE WISE MEN

1

KINDER'S SOUTHERN EDGE—10 MILES

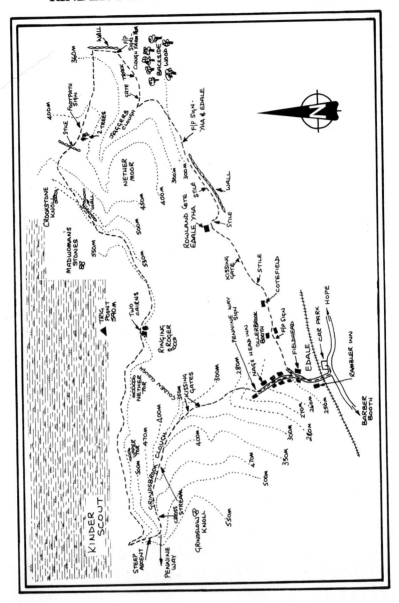

KINDER & BLEAKLOW—Huge moorland areas which in summer provide relatively easy walking in good visibility. In autumn, winter and spring the walking becomes more serious and, although often on good paths, you should be properly shod, have good rain-gear and be proficient in map and compass work. It is not an area to be taken lightly. Across both, the Pennine Way begins its journey to Scotland. From the 'Glorious Twelfth'—August 12th—grouse shooting takes place on the moors, and notices at the entry points give details of which moors are closed on specific days.

LONG CIRCULAR WALKS
IN THE
PEAK DISTRICT

by

JOHN N. MERRILL

Maps and Photographs by John N. Merrill

A J.N.M. PUBLICATION

1986

A J.N.M. PUBLICATION

J.N.M. PUBLICATIONS,
WINSTER,
MATLOCK,
DERBYSHIRE, DE4 2DQ.

Conceived, edited,typset and designed by John N. Merrill

A J.N.M. Publication

© Copyright—Text and Routes—John N. Merrill 1986
© Copyright—Maps and Photographs—John N. Merrill 1986

First Published—August 1983

Reprinted—1984 and 1985

This revised and enlarged edition set in Plantin – September 1986

ISBN 0 907496 42 3

Typesetting interfaced by:
Steve Rothwell Typesetting Services, 20 St Ann's Square, Manchester, M2 7HG

Printed by Adams & Sons (Printers) Ltd., Blueschool Street, Hereford

J.N.M. Publications, Winster, Derbyshire, DE4 2DQ.

John Merrill.

ABOUT JOHN N. MERRILL

John combines the characteristics and strength of a mountain climber with the stamina, and athletic capabilities of a marathon runner. In this respect he is unique and has to his credit a whole string of remarkable long walks. He is without question the world's leading marathon walker.

Over the last ten years he has walked more than 55,000 miles and successfully completed ten walks of at least 1,000 miles or more.

His six walks in Britain are—

Hebridean Journey ....1,003 miles
Northern Isles Journey.......................................913 miles
Irish Island Journey ....1,578 miles
Parkland Journey ....2,043 miles
Lands End to John O'Groats ....1,608 miles

and in 1978 he became the first person (permanent Guinness Book Of Records entry) to walk the entire coastline of Britain—6,824 miles in ten months.

In Europe he has walked across Austria (712 miles), hiked the Tour of Mont Blanc and GR20 in Corsica as training! In 1982 he walked across Europe—2,806 miles in 107 days—crossing seven countries, the Swiss and French Alps and the complete Pyrennean chain—the hardest and longest mountain walk in Europe.

In America he used the world's longest footpath—The Appalachian Trail (2,200 miles) as a training walk. The following year he walked from Mexico to Canada in record time—118 days for 2,700 miles.

During the summer of 1984, John set off from Virginia Beach on the Atlantic coast, and walked 4,226 miles without a rest day, across the width of America to San Francisco and the Pacific Ocean. This walk is unquestionably his greatest achievement, being, in modern history, the longest, hardest crossing of the USA in the shortest time—under six months (177 days). The direct distance is 2,800 miles.

Between major walks John is out training in his own area —the Peak District National Park. As well as walking in other areas of Britain and in Europe he has been trekking in the Himalayas four times. He lectures extensively and is author of more than sixty books.

CONTENTS

EDALE CROSS

WALK NO 1—
KINDER'S SOUTHERN EDGE—
10 miles—allow 4½ hours

BASIC ROUTE—*Edale—Grindsbrook—Edale Moor—Nether Tor—Druid's Stone—Jaggers Clough—Crookstone Hill—Jaggers Clough— Rowland Cote(Edale Youth Hostel)*

MAP—*1:25,000 Outdoor Leisure Map—The Dark Peak.*

CAR PARK—*Edale—junction of village road and Hope/Barber Booth road.*

ABOUT THE WALK—A short walk along the perimeter of the Kinder plateau. All on a well—defined path. After the initial climb it is descending almost all the way! The views on a clear day are extensive.

WALKING INSTRUCTIONS—From the car park turn right and walk up the village road onto Edale, passing the Rambler Inn on your left and Fieldshead campsite and information centre on your right. Continue on the road past the Nag's Head Inn on your right. At the entrance gates to Grindslow House, a few yards later, turn right on to the 'Pennine Way', and descend to the footbridge across the stream. Ascend the steps and follow the well-worn path up Grindsbrook. ¼ mile later pass through two kissing gates before reaching 'Open Country'. Continue ahead on the path with the brook on your left. ½ mile later cross to the lefthand side of the brook as you steadily ascend. In another ½ mile cross to your right and begin the final steep ascent to the plateau rim. Here turn right and follow the well-defined path around the perimeter. At first you look down on your upward path before walking along the top of Nether Tor. Continue ahead across the spur of Ringing Roger and an open gritstone area, passing two large cairns. ¼ mile later keep to the lefthand path as you contour round just beneath the moorland rim—on your left. On your immediate right is a stone wall. A further ¼ mile and you are heading due north to the crossing of Jaggers Clough. You keep another wall on your right before reaching a large boulder. Here you turn right and descend from the plateau, first following path then track over Crookstone Hill. At the wall is a stile beside the gate before crossing the subsequent field to two solitary trees. Here, as footpath signposted, turn left and follow the path down the field to a wall, stile on your right, and boundary sign for 'Open Country'.

Turn right over the stile and walk along the grass track beside the wall to a crossroads of paths with sign. Don't ascend the stile—turn right on the path/track towards 'Clough Farm 1½ miles'. After 150 yards the track descends to Jaggers Clough. Cross the stream and through the gate, entering Ashop Moor National Trust property. Follow the track as it swings right then sharply left up the clough side. Keep on the well-used path for the next ½ mile to a footpath sign. Here turn right following the path—Youth Hostel and Edale. Keep the wall on your left and soon descend to a small stream before ascending and curving round to the Youth Hostel. The path is well signed as you walk round in front of the building to a kissing gate. Keep on across the field, ascending gently along a grass trackway. ¼ mile later, beside an 'open country' sign, you descend to your left down the path to a stile. Here turn right and walk past Cotefield and its farmyard. ¼ mile later reach the farms of Ollerbrook Booth. Go past the houses and gate to the second farm road on your left. Here, as footpath-signposted, turn left and follow the track to Edale, skirting the camping-ground of Fieldhead. Turn left at the road and retrace your steps back to the car-park.

THE PENNINE WAY ALTERNATIVE—12 MILES

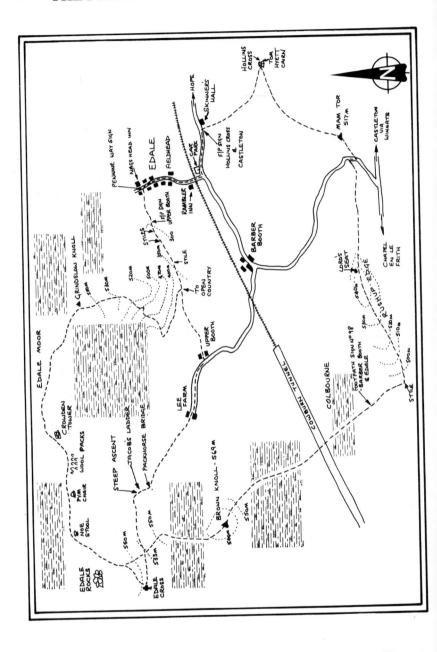

of Mam Tor. Descend the ridge to Hollins Cross just over ½ mile away. Here you leave the ridge and descend the well worn path past Hollins Farm to the road near Skinner's Hall, ½ mile away. At the road turn left and ¼ mile later you are back at the car park.

WALK NO 2—
THE PENNINE WAY ALTERNATIVE
12 Miles—allow 5/6 hours

BASIC ROUTE—*Edale—Upper Booth—Lee Farm—Jacob's Ladder—Brown Knoll—Colborne—Rushup Edge—Mam Tor—Hollins Cross—Edale.*

MAPS—*1:25,000 Outdoor Leisure Map—The Dark Peak.*

CAR PARK—*Edale; at the junction of the village road and Hope road.*

ABOUT THE WALK—The first half of the walk follows the line of the alternative start of the Pennine Way from Edale onto Kinder Scout via Jacob's Ladder. Instead of following this route, you can ascend into open country and walk around the southern edge of Kinder and join the route near Edale Cross onto Brown Knoll. The walk encircles the head of the Vale of Edale, providing extensive views over hills and moorland.

WALKING INSTRUCTIONS—Turn right out of the car park and walk up the village road into Edale, passing the Rambler Inn on your left; Fieldhead Information Centre and campsite on your right. Just before the Old Nags Head Inn turn left onto the signposted path—Pennine Way. At first this is in a shallow ditch. After 200 yards turn left over the stile and follow the signposted path—Upper Booth. The path is well defined as you cross the well-stiled fields. ½ mile later, on the highest point of the path at the junction of the path on your right into 'open country', you descend gently down to Upper Booth. If you are taking the alternative 'High Level Route', you turn right and follow the path onto Kinder's plateau edge.

Turn left and descend to the farmyard in Upper Booth. At the road turn right and walk along it into National Trust property—Lee Farm. Walk through the farm, ¼ mile later, passing a National Trust information centre on your left. Continue ahead on the track, and in ½ mile you reach the packhorse bridge. Cross and begin the steep ascent to your right of Jacob's Ladder, en route passing the boundary of 'Open Country' and footpath sign No. 97—'Jacob's Ladder to Hayfield'. At the top of the main ascent you reach footpath sign No. 85—'Edale'. Continue on the well-worn path and ascend more gently now, passing a large cairn, and in ¼ mile the path on your right to the Kinder Plateau—(this is the path you descend if you have been on the 'High Level Route'). Just beyond this righthand path—you keep to the lefthand one—you reach a metal Pennine Way sign. Here you leave this route and turn left, following a path beside a wall on your right. Follow this path for the next ¾ mile as you cross moorland, which in most seasons is quite boggy. The path is defined, and after ½ mile you leave the wallside and head directly for the white triangulation pillar. In bad weather compass bearings are a useful precaution over this moorland. From the pillar you head south easterly, still following a defined path which gets better once away from the pillar. For the next 1¾ miles you cross Colbourne moorland and the Cowburn Tunnel. In good weather the walk across here is excellent and presents no route-finding problems. After 1¾ miles you have been walking close to a ruined wall before reaching footpath sign No. 98—'Barber Booth and Edale'. Don't descend, but keep straight ahead on the path with the wall on your left. After ½ mile you have a fence for company as you curve round to your right to a stile and track. Ascend the stile and walk along the track on your left. This takes you first past a tumulus, where a triangulation used to be, before you descend gradually along the crest of Rushup Edge. The path is well used and stiled. Upon reaching the road in front of Mam Tor, turn right then left over the stile and ascend the many steps to the summit

KINDER DOWNFALL—12 MILES

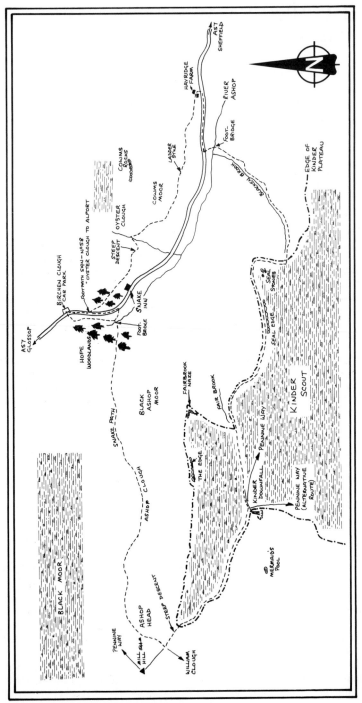

WALK NO 3—KINDER DOWNFALL—
12 Miles—allow 5/6 hours

BASIC ROUTE—*Snake Inn—Course of Roman Road—Oyster Clough—Hayridge Farm—River Ashop—Blackden Brook—Seal Edge—Fair Brook—Kinder Scout—Kinder Downfall—Pennine Way—Ashop Head—Snake Path—Ashop Clough—Snake Inn.*

MAP—*1:25,000 O.S. Outdoor Leisure Map—The Dark Peak.*

CAR PARK—*Birchin Clough—Grid Ref SK109914*

ABOUT THE WALK—Kinder Downfall is one of the most spectacular sights of the Dark Peak. This walk takes you by a less popular route to the Downfall and is along footpaths, except for the short crossing of Kinder Scout from Fair Brook to the Downfall. It is the shortest crossing on Kinder, but a compass is essential. The ascent onto Kinder via Blackden Brook is extremely pleasant, and the path via Oyster Clough gives you excellent views of the Kinder Plateau.

WALKING INSTRUCTIONS—Walk down the Snake Road—A57—to the path sign on your left—No. 58—'Oyster Clough to Alport'. First ascend through the pine trees for just over ¼ mile to a stile and boundary of Open Country. Continue ahead on the path with the trees on your right. At the top of the rise you descend to your right then left to the stream in the bottom of Oyster Clough. Cross this and ascend the path to your right, with the wall on your right. The pathline is discernible and well-stiled. After the initial ascent the path levels off for ¼ mile to a ladder stile at another boundary of Open Countryside. Here the path descends to Hayridge Farm. Just before it, bear left beside the wall and walk round the farm to the track before turning right along the track through the farm to the A57 road.

Turn right along the road for just over ¼ mile to the path on your left that descends to the River Ashop. Cross the footbridge and just beyond enter open country. The path is well-defined as you begin ascending above Blackden Brook. After almost 1½ miles of ascent you reach the rim of Kinder Scout. Turn right first for Seal Stones before walking around the edge of Kinder along Seal Edge to the top of Fair Brook, 1¼ miles away. Here you leave the Edge and on compass bearing cross the moorland and groughs for Kinder Downfall, ½ mile away. Before you reach the Downfall you will gain the wide river channel which you follow to the Fall. Here you join the Pennine Way.

Turn right at the Downfall and follow the well-worn Pennine Way around the western edge of Kinder for 1¼ miles. Descend the short but steep slope to Ashop Head. Here leave the Pennine Way and follow the Snake Path down Ashop Clough for the next three miles to the footbridge over the stream. Bear right then left, and ascend to the A57 road and path sign. The Snake Inn is just down the road on your right and the car park is up the road, ¼ mile away.

KINDER DOWNFALL

AROUND BLEAKLOW—20 MILES

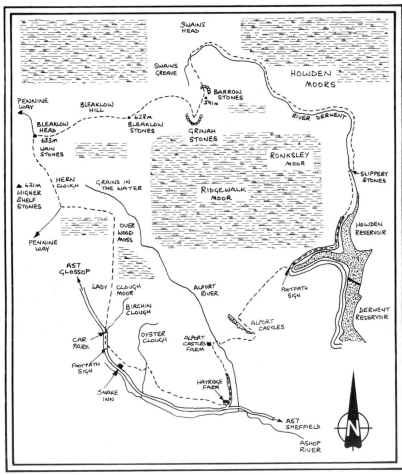

OPEN COUNTRY SIGN

WALK NO 4—AROUND BLEAKLOW—
20 Miles—allow 8/9 hours

BASIC ROUTE—*Birchin Clough—Over Wood Moss—Alport Low—Pennine Way—Bleaklow Head—Bleaklow Hill—Bleaklow Stones—Grinah Stones—Barrow Stones —River Derwent—Slippery Stones—Howden Reservoir—Ditch Clough Plantation—Alport Castles—Alport Castles Farm—Hayridge Farm—Course of Roman Road—Birchin Clough.*

MAP—*1:25,000 O.S. Outdoor Leisure Map—The Dark Peak.*

CAR PARK—*Birchin Clough. Grid Ref SK109914.*

ABOUT THE WALK—The toughest walk in the book, where expert map reading and compass work is essential. In summer there should be little problem finding your way, but in winter or misty weather the crossing of Bleaklow can be hard. Despite the severity of the route, which includes numerous ascents and descents, the walk is a magnificent circuit through some of the wildest scenery in the Peak District. Allow eight hours.

WALKING INSTRUCTIONS—From the car park ascend the forest path, which is steep and has numerous steps. At the end of the trees ascend a ladder stile and continue ascending a path which soon peters out. A few yards later you reach the perimeter of Lady Clough Moor, and the initial cruel ascent is over. Head almost due north across the grassy moorland, keeping to the high ground for the next 1¼ miles over 'Over Wood Moss' to the head of Upper North Grain. Here turn left and heading almost due west—still no path—for the next ¾ mile, until you reach the wooden stakes and the well-trodden Pennine Way. Turn right and keep to the line of the Pennine Way for the next mile. At Hern Clough keep to the right path that hugs the stream. Pass Hern Stones and onto Bleaklow Head and the Wain Stones. Here you leave the Pennine Way and turn right, almost due east at first for Bleaklow Hill. A path is now becoming work over the peat groughs and the wooden stakes; many marked with H 09 help to guide you. A mile—about ½ an hour's walking—will bring you to Bleaklow Hill. Again heading almost due east, follow the path and

SNAKE INN

9

stakes for just over ½ mile to Bleaklow Stones. Your next object is Grinah Stones, a mile away. There is a path to them, and it goes beneath the high moorland edge, curving round the upper reaches of Deep Grain. Grinah Stones has several imposing rocks. From here turn left—almost due north to Barrow Stones ½ mile away. From these Stones you leave the high moorland and descend the eastern side of Swains Greave—the start of the River Derwent. On the left-hand side of the infant river is a faint path. Follow this for the next four miles; the path becoming more prominent the farther you go.

After about 1½ miles, the path becomes a track and you follow this to Slippery Stones. Cross the packhorse bridge which once stood in Derwent Village. Continue on the wide track to the road end ¾ mile away. Follow the road beside Howden Reservoir for the next mile to the end of the righthand arm of the reservoir. Here is the stile and signposted path—'Alport Castle; to Hope and Edale'. Follow the track for 200 yards to another footpath sign. Here turn left and ascend the steep track through Ditch Clough Plantation. At the end of the trees you reach 'open country' once more. Follow the track ahead as it gently ascends on the right of Ditch Clough. After ½ mile a wall on your right keeps you company before reaching the edge of Alport Castles. Turn left here and follow the path along the edge for ¼ mile before descending along the path down to Alport Dale, ½ mile away. Cross the Alport River via the footbridge and bear right then left into Alport Castles Farm. Join the farm track, passing Alport Camping Barn on your right, and follow the track for just over a mile to Hayridge Farm. Just before the farm, at the metal signpost, turn right around the farm—'Oyster Clough to Glossop'.

Around the farm follow an ascending grass track with a wall on your left. The whole route is well-stiled, and after ½ mile you reach a ladder stile and 'open country'. Continue with the wall on your left for a further ¼ mile before leaving it and heading for a wooden stile. 150 yards beyond the stile, another wall keeps you company as you descend to Oyster Clough. Cross the stream and ascend the path, which swings to your left then right beside the trees. Keep the trees on your left before following a path well away from them to a stile and another boundary sign of 'Open Country'. Cross the stile into the trees, and keep to the righthand path through them before descending to the Snake Road—A57—¼ mile away. Turn right, and 150 yards up the road you reach the car park.

THE ALPORT VALLEY

HOWDEN RESERVOIR

HOPE VALLEY—HIGH LEVEL ROUTE—13 MILES

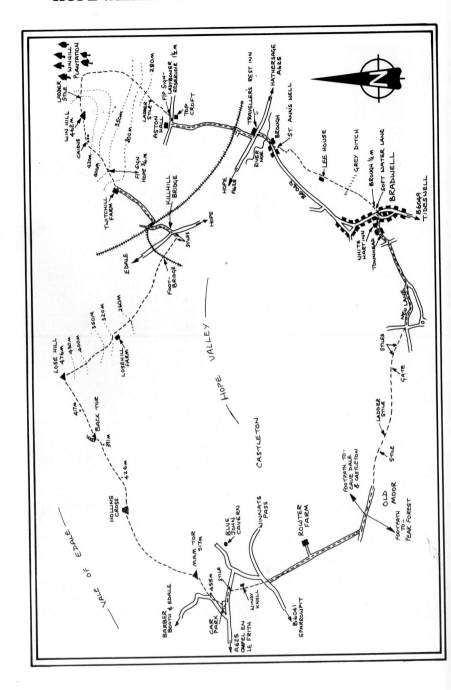

HOPE VALLEY—HIGH LEVEL ROUTE
13 Miles—allow 5/6 hours

BASIC ROUTE—*Mam Tor car park—Windy Knoll—Old Moor—Bradwell—Brough—Aston—Win Hill—Townhead—Losehill Farm—Lose Hill—Back Tor—Hollins Cross—Mam Tor—car park.*

MAP—*1:25,000 O.S. Outdoor Leisure Map—The Dark Peak.*

CAR PARK—*Close to junction of A625 and Barber Booth road, beneath Mam Tor.*

ABOUT THE WALK—The grand circuit along the Peak District's finest ridge, with magnificent views over the valley and to Kinder and Derwent. Whilst the ridge is gritstone, the other side of the valley—Old Moor—is limestone country. You descend through Bradwell, a very attractive limestone village. Near Brough, and at the start of the first real climb, is an aptly-named inn—The Travellers Rest.

WALKING INSTRUCTIONS—At the entrance to the car park turn left, 200 yards later turn right over the stile and follow the path to your right, through Windy Knoll; National Trust property. At the road, almost ½ mile later, (B6061), cross over to the metal gate and tarmaced track for Rowter Farm (campside). Ascend the track and, at the entrance to the farm ½ mile later, keep straight ahead to a gate and the now rough track. A further ½ mile along the walled track turn left, still on the track. At the crossroads of paths, just beyond, keep straight on the track, signposted 'Batham Gate 1 mile'. At a small quarry go through the stile and continue on the track, curving around to your right around the spoil heaps. 150 yards later, where the track turns sharp left, keep straight ahead over the stile and head for another stile before reaching a ladder stile. For the next mile you head almost due east as you follow a faint path, but all the stiles—mostly ladder type—indicate the way. In the final stages, just after your first gate, you bear right and cross two stiles to gain the crossroads. Go straight across onto 'New Lane'—a walled track. Follow this gently-descending track to a tarmaced road ½ mile later. Turn left and keep straight ahead, now descending more steeply as you reach the fringe of Bradwell. Continue straight ahead as you descend 'Townhead', passing shops and the White Hart Inn on your left. At the bottom bear left along 'Bridge Street' to the main road—B6049—beside the Bradwell Ice Cream Shop. Turn right and left almost immediately along 'Soft Water Lane'. After 100 yards bear right onto the path signposted—'Brough ½ mile'. It is much further than that! The path is quite well-defined and very well stiled. At each stile you can see ahead to the next, making route finding simple. Cross Grey Ditch, pass Lee House, and three fields later keep the field boundary on your immediate right to reach the stiles and signposts as the path goes around the perimeter fence of a works before you gain St. Ann's Well built in 1859, at Brough. Turn left to the B6049 road and turn right to the A625 road and the Travellers Rest Inn.

Ascend the road to 'Aston' on the left of the inn, for the next mile. At the road junction in front of Aston Hall and Farm, turn right. A few yards later, and just past 'Top Croft' on your right, turn left onto a signposted path—'Ladybower Reservoir 1½ miles'. Begin ascending up a field to a stile and then more steeply to a ladder stile and footpath sign—'Win Hill'. Continue ascending this to the Winhill Plantation. Turn left and ascend the wide path through the sparse plantation to a ladder stile and the final slope to Win Hill summit. Traverse the summit, and at the third large cairn turn left and begin descending on a distinct path. Ascend a ladder stile and descend more steeply to a stile and footpath sign—'Hope ¾ mile'. Descend again to the ruins of Twitchell Farm. Here descend the farm track and follow it to your right through the trees to the road in front of the railway bridge. Turn left and follow the road to Killhill Bridge and Edale road. Cross the road to the stile on the immediate right of the white house. Pass through two more stiles before turning right to another stile and begin heading for Lose Hill. The path is well stiled and leads you first of all to a footbridge over the railway. Continue ahead past a house on your left to a crossroads of paths. Keep straight ahead on the 'Lose Hill' signposted path. A little later, as you now start to ascend gradually, you reach another stile and path sign. It states Lose Hill is 2 miles—quite wrong—it is 2 miles from here to Mam Tor! A further sign is reached—No. 93—'Lose Hill and Mam Tor'. Ascend to the righthand side of Losehill Farm, bearing left around it before ascending again for Lose Hill summit, passing a large cairn on your right.

Upon the summit of Lose Hill a large panorama plaque details the viewpoints. Having now gained the crest of the Peakland Ridge, simply walk along following its undulations to the summit of Back Tor, Hollins Cross and its cairn in memory of Tom Hyett and onto the summit of Mam Tor. Descend the other side down the steps to the road. Bear right down this before turning left and descending back into the car park.

The walk can also be done by starting from near Brough, thus enabling you to get the ascents over first while still fresh, leaving the easy but pleasant walk over Old Moor to unwind at the end.

MAM TOR

14

LOSE HILL PATH SIGN

WINNATS PASS

SILLY DALE—15 MILES

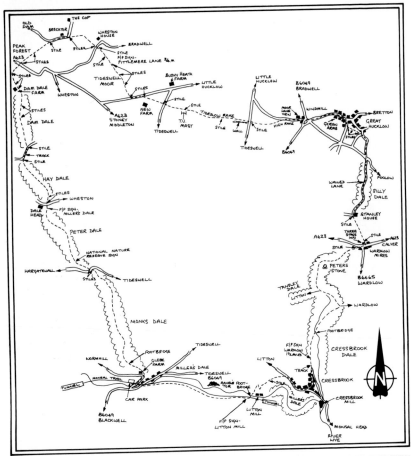

RAVENSDALE IN CRESSBROOK DALE

WALK NO 6—
SILLY DALE—*15 Miles—allow 6/7 hours*

BASIC ROUTE—*Miller's Dale Car Park—Monsal Trail—Litton Mill—Cressbrook—Cressbrook Dale—Wardlow Mires—Stanley House—Silly Dale—Grindlow—Great Hucklow—Windmill—High Rake—Tideslow Rake—Tideswell Moor—Brocktor—Dam Dale Farm—Dam Dale—Hay Dale—Peter Dale—Monk's Dale—Gleve Farm—Miller's Dale Car Park.*

MAP—*1:25,000 O.S. Outdoor Leisure Map—The White Peak.*

CAR PARK—*Miller's Dale Station.*

ABOUT THE WALK—A walk through the limestone country of the Peak District; including traversing seven dales. Much of the route lies in unspoilt scenery rarely walked, and you see few people. Interspersed with the route are attractive villages and distant views on the limestone plateau region of the National Park.

WALKING INSTRUCTIONS—Turn left onto the Monsal Trail and walk along it for 1¼ miles to the path sign for Litton Mill. Turn left and descend the path to the footbridge over the River Wye. At the houses turn right to the entrance to Litton Mill. Go through the entrance and turn left up the track. After 50 yards you reach a footpath sign on your right. Keep straight ahead to a stile and ascend the track beyond, following it to your right then left up the dale side. After the initial ascent keep to the righthand grass track to a walled track and stile. Walk up the track to the road and turn right, passing a chapel on your left. Bear left 150 yards later down the road, passing the houses of Cressbrook Village. At the Methodist Chapel just beyond, keep to the lefthand road. Where the road turns abruptly right, keep straight ahead on a track through the wood. After 150 yards you pass a footpath sign—'Wardlow 1½ miles'. Afterwards emerge into open country and descend, keeping the stone wall and wood on your left. ¼ mile later cross a footbridge and begin ascending the path up the dale side. ½ mile later at the top turn left and descend the path down to the dale floor at the junction of Tansley Dale. Continue along the floor of Cressbrook Dale, passing Peter's Stone on your right. Just before the road junction at Wardlow Mires, cross a stile and walk in front of a small cottage.

At the road turn right along the A623 road, and just past the Three Stags Head Inn turn left through the farm to a stile behind the buildings. Keep the wall on your left as you cross the fields to the stile on the right of Stanley House. Walk past the house on the walled track, and ¼ mile later turn left onto another walled path and follow this for the next ½ mile with Silly Dale on your right. At the road from Foolow cross over and walk into Grindlow village. Turn left and at the next road, 100 yards later, turn left to the stile and path on your right. Cross four well-stiled fields to the road. Turn right into Great Hucklow village. Opposite the shop turn left along the road through the village and past the Queens Arms. At the road junction ¼ mile later turn right and cross another road and walk past the houses of Windmill, passing Moor Lane View. ¼ mile later leave the lane and follow a track on your left. At the bar gate 50 yards later bear right and follow the track to a minor road. Cross over to the stile and keep the wall on your left as you ascend gently along Tideslow Rake. After a mile, at the highest point of the path, with the TV mast well to your left, pass through a stile before walking around opencast workings to a gate and minor road. Cross the road to a stile and cross the stiled fields on the right of New Farm. At the minor road turn left, and after 50 yards, with a stile on your left, turn right over a stile and begin crossing the well-stiled fields of Tideswell Moor. ¾ mile later you ascend a ladder stile to a road near Wheston House and path sign—'Pittlemere Lane

¾ mile'. As footpath-signed, cross a stile and field to another stile where you bear left and walk close to a solitary millstone to reach a gate and stile beside the lane at Brocktor. Walk down the road for 120 yards, and in front of the first house on your left go through the stile and descend the field with the wall on your right. At the bottom ascend two stiles and keep the wall on your left as you ascend to the road—A623 to the right of Laneside Farm.

Cross the road and cross the field, keeping the wall on your right. At the first stile on your right, turn left to a stile and descend the next field to a stile. Walk past Dam Dale Farm, keeping it on your right. Beyond, walk along Dam Dale, keeping the wall on your right. After ¾ mile ascend a stile onto a track. Turn right and follow this for 150 yards to a stile on your left and the start of Hay Dale. Walk along this dale for ¾ mile to the minor road at Dale Head. Cross the road to your right to the stile and follow the footpath down Peter's Dale. After a mile along the dale floor you pass a National Nature Reserve sign—'Derbyshire Dales'—and gain the minor road from Tideswell. Cross this road and follow the path—rocky at first—through Monk's Dale. After a mile the path leaves the dale floor and ascends to your left before contouring round above the small stream. A little over ¼ mile later you descend to a footbridge over the stream before turning left and ascending up the righthand side of the dale. At the top turn right for Glebe Farm. Ascend the stile and reach the Wormhill road. Turn left and descend to the car park at Miller's Dale Station on your right.

REMEMBER AND OBSERVE THE COUNTRY CODE

ENJOY THE COUNTRYSIDE AND RESPECT ITS LIFE AND WORK.

GUARD AGAINST ALL RISK OF FIRE.

FASTEN ALL GATES.

KEEP YOUR DOGS UNDER CLOSE CONTROL.

KEEP TO PUBLIC PATHS ACROSS FARMLAND.

USE GATES AND STILES TO CROSS FENCES, HEDGES AND WALLS.

LEAVE LIVESTOCK, CROPS AND MACHINERY ALONE.

TAKE YOUR LITTER HOME—PACK IT IN, PACK IT OUT.

HELP TO KEEP ALL WATER CLEAN.

PROTECT WILDLIFE, PLANTS AND TREES.

TAKE SPECIAL CARE ON COUNTRY ROADS.

MAKE NO UNNECESSARY NOISE.

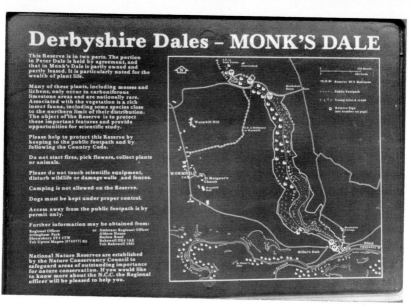

NATURE RESERVE NOTICE

PETER DALE

19

BAKEWELL AND STANTON MOOR—15 MILES

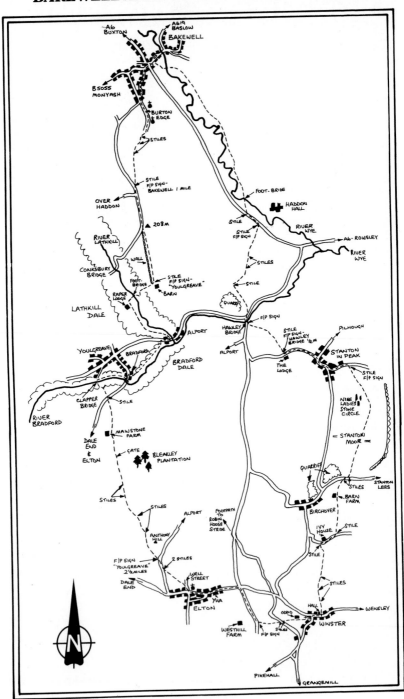

WALK NO 7—
BAKEWELL AND STANTON MOOR—
15 Miles—allow 6/7 hours

BASIC ROUTE—*Bakewell—Haddon Fields—River Lathkill—Alport—Bradford—Mawstone Farm—Elton—Winster—Stanton Moor—Stanton in Peak—Hawley's Bridge—River Wye—Bakewell.*

MAP—*1:25,000 O.S. Outdoor Leisure Map—The White Peak.*

CAR PARK—*Central Bakewell.*

ABOUT THE WALK—First you traverse the limestone plateau to the River Lathkill before ascending into gritstone country around Elton and Stanton. You descend into limestone again near Haddon Hall. The route takes you into scenically popular areas but along paths little used, providing distant views of moor, dales and halls.

WALKING INSTRUCTIONS—From Rutland Square in Bakewell, walk up the Monyash road—King Street, on the immediate left of the Rutland Arms. Turn left along Butts Road, and follow this to its end and ascend the tarmaced path and steps. At the top turn left and walk along 'Burton Edge' past the cemetery on your left. Continue ahead on the track which soon descends to a stile. Bear right and follow the well-stiled path as it ascends across the fields to the road near Norton Barn Farm, ½ mile away. Turn left and walk along the road for ½ mile. Where it turns sharp right, keep straight ahead on a path, with the wall on your immediate right. At the end of the second field and just before the farm building turn right, through a stile, footpath signposted—'Youlgreave'. Cross a wooden stile and descend the path through the trees to a footbridge over the River Lathkill. Turn left just afterwards along the well-used and stiled path to Alport, ½ mile away.

Turn right at the road in Alport and, after 100 yards and opposite an electric light post, is the stile and path high above the River Bradford. Simply maintain height as you cross the fields to Bradford, ½ mile away. You reach the road here on the right of Braemar House. Turn left and descend to the river. Turn right and follow the path on the right of the river for the next ¼ mile. Upon reaching a minor road from Youlgreave, cross the river via a clapper bridge and turn left and ascend out of the dale via a well-used path. Cross a stile at the top and descend to the road. Turn right and left almost immediately, and walk along the drive towards Mawstone Farm. Just before the first gate, turn right to a stile and begin ascending to the left of the farm. Keep left beyond it, following the farm track through woodland and past a barn on your right. Go through a further gate and, just before the next, you leave the track to your right to another gate. Here you gain the line of a footpath as you cross a field to a stile and narrow wood. Four more stiles bring you near a pine hillock; before which you bear left, via more stiles and past gritstone outcrops on your left. The path curves right to yet more stiles as you aim for the right of a prominent quarry. Walk on the immediate right of this, on a well-used path, to the minor road to Elton and footpath sign—'Youlgreave 2 ½ miles'.

Turn right and descend the road for 150 yards to two stiles and path sign—'Elton'. Cross the stiles and ascend the two fields to Elton, reached via Well Street and passing the church. Turn left and walk along the Main Street, which is soon named Winster Lane. 250 yards beyond the houses you reach a small crossroads, turn right onto the farm track and follow this for a little over ¼ mile to a stile on your right and footpath sign. Cross five stiles to the minor road. Cross this to the stile on your right and cross three fields to reach Winster via the churchyard. Turn left, then right, into Winster's main street. Just past the Hall, turn left as footpath-signposted—'Birchover 1 mile'. The path is not too well-defined, but it is well-stiled and in places it is stone flagged. First you descend, before ascending steeply on the right of a well-eroded cattle track. At the top turn left and then right around the wall to the stile on the left of Ivy House. Turn right past the house on the track and a field later on your left is the stile and path. Follow this path close to the stone wall on your left. Walk past the righthand side of Barn Farm, passing through a gate. At the top of the field a stile leads you onto the road from Birchover. Cross this and walk onto Stanton Moor via the stile, wide track and ancient monument sign—'Stanton Moor Stone Circle ¾ mile'. After 100 yards keep to the lefthand track and cross the moorland to the circle and onto the road, ½ mile later. Turn left and descend the road into Stanton village, passing the church and inn. One mile down the road and opposite a lodge to Stanton Hall, turn right as footpath-signposted—'Hawley's Bridge ½ mile'. Cross the field to a stile before walking along a hawthorn-hedged path. In due course you descend through the trees to the road close to the bridge. Turn right and cross the Youlgreave road—B5056—and ascend the track beyond on the right of a large quarry. A little over ¼ mile, close to a dew pond, pass through a stile by a gate to another stile on your right. Cross the field to the righthand side of a wood, before crossing another field to a stile and the descent to the A6 road opposite the entrance to Haddon Hall. Turn left, and 300 yards later on your right is the stile and signposted path for Bakewell. Walk along the walled path, across the River Wye, to a track. Turn right then left and follow the well-used path on the right of the River Wye all the way back to Bakewell. In the final stages cross two footbridges to enter central Bakewell.

EARL GREY TOWER, STANTON MOOR

22

COURTYARD, HADDON HALL

LATHKILL DALE

THE MONSAL TRAIL—18 MILES

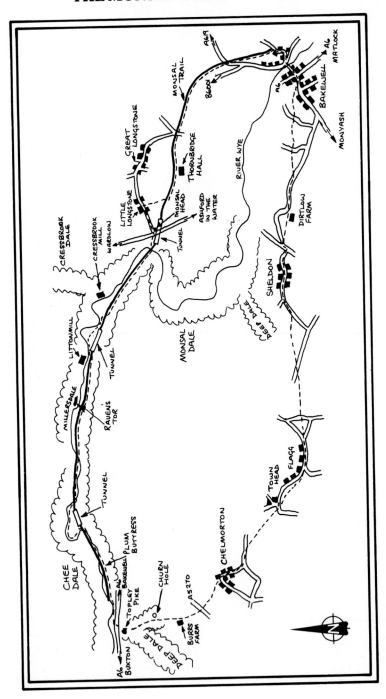

WALK NO 8—THE MONSAL TRAIL—
18 Miles—allow 7/8 hours

BASIC ROUTE—*Bakewell—Monsal Trail—Little Longstone—Monsal Head—Miller's Dale—Chee Dale—Topley Pike Quarry—Churn Hole—Chelmorton—Flagg—Sheldon—Dirtlow Farm—Bakewell.*

MAP—*1:25,000 Outdoor Leisure Map—The White Peak.*

CAR PARK—*Central Bakewell.*

ABOUT THE WALK—A walk along the entire length of the Monsal Trail, the Peak District's newest trail. Because of several long tunnels, it is necessary to deviate off the trail and use footpaths to link it all together. The path above Miller's Dale is for the 'sure-footed' only, but is by far the best 'alpine style path' in the area. After the trail you traverse the limestone plateau via many unspoilt villages.

WALKING INSTRUCTIONS—Walk along the main street in Bakewell from the Rutland Arms Hotel, past the Information Office on your right over the five-arched bridge over the River Wye. Turn half right and ascend Station Road. Just past Burre Close on your left, enter the small industrial estate and gain the Monsal Trail. Follow the trail for the next three miles. Shortly after Thornbridge Station, as signposted, leave the trail and follow the well-used and stiled path across the fields to Little Longstone. Turn left and walk through the village, passing the Packhorse Inn on your right (backpackers welcome) and ascend gently to Monsal Head. Cross the road, and on the right opposite the house on your left is the stile and path sign for rejoining the trail. Turn left and rejoin the trail in '50 yards'. Continue along the trail and the famous viaduct across Monsal Dale. ¼ mile later, a sign states that the route ahead is only for the 'sure-footed'. If exposed heights worry you turn left and descend the road to Upperdale Farm and follow the road to your left to Cressbrook Mill. Walk through Miller's Dale, and at Litton Mill you can rejoin the trail on your left. For those on the 'sure-footed' way, continue along the trail and, just before the closed tunnel built in 1835, turn right onto the concessionary path. You gain the trail a mile later near Litton Mill.

Continue along the trail into Miller's Dale Station (toilets). ¼ mile later leave the trail via the path on your right and descend into Chee Dale. Upon reaching the River Wye by a footbridge, turn left and keep the river on your immediate left. The path is well-defined as you curve round the dale past Chee Tor and across the stepping stones. Shortly afterwards, cross to the other side of the river via the footbridge. A few yards more and, as signposted, you regain the trail for the last time. You pass under two small tunnels before passing Plum Buttress on your left—at 270 feet high it is the highest limestone buttress in the Peak District. 150 yards later you descend from the trail to the track which takes you to Wye Dale car park and the A6 road. Cross the road and, as footpath signposted, 'Chelmorton' —walk along the lefthand side of Topley Pike Quarry. The path is readily defined. Bear left after ¼ mile and walk up a shallow dale to Churn Hole, ascending out of the dale via its righthand side. Cross the stile at the top and keep straight ahead across the fields and stiles to Burr's Farm. Beyond, walk along a walled grass track to the A5270 road. Cross over and as signposted—'Main Street ½ mile' —follow the farm track into Chelmorton village. At the Main Street the Church Inn is on your left.

Cross the Main Street and follow the minor road out of the village. ½ mile later, at the road T-junction, turn left—'Flagg 1 ½ miles'. 150 yards later turn right over the stile, on the signposted footpath. The pathline is faint, but the route is well-stiled for the next ¾ mile to High Stool Farm, which you pass on your immediate right to gain a minor road. Cross this to the stile and cross several more well-stiled fields to Flagg village on your left. Turn right after the stile and walk along the road, passing the shop/post office on your left. Keep to the road as it bears left past Flagg Hall and the Plough Inn. Just after the inn, turn right onto the Monyash Road. After 50 yards leave it on your left via a stile underneath a pine tree. Cross three more stiles to reach another minor road. Go straight across this to the next stile and path sign—'Sheldon'. Again the path is not defined but well-stiled. After the first field the next stile is on the right of an electricity pole. After ½ mile you reach a minor road opposite the entrance to Deep Dale. Turn right along this road, and after 75 yards, on your left, is the stile and path to Sheldon, now 1 mile away. Cross further stiled fields, reaching the Sheldon road to the left of Johnson Lane Farm. Turn left and walk along the road over the brow of the hill and down through Sheldon village, which alas has no shop or inn!

Continue along the road out of the village and down into Kirk Dale. Where the road turns sharp right is a stile on your left, and you descend the field to the road, cutting the corner. Turn left, then right, up the minor road. At the top end of the small wood on your right is the stile steps. Ascend a field to a wall, which you keep on your left as you descend to the immediate left of Dirtlow Farm. Cross the farm track and descend the field to the road bend, stile and path sign. Turn right and follow the road for almost ½ mile. Opposite a barn on your right is the stile and footpath sign. You are now heading due east as you cross the stiled fields to a minor road. Cross this and ascend the field beyond with the wall on your right. Bear left in the next field before continuing straight ahead across two more fields. Cross a minor road to two stiles and descend further fields to the outskirts of Bakewell; all the time the church spire acts as a guide. Descend Parsonage Croft and the churchyard into Bakewell.

MONSAL DALE

BAKEWELL: RIVER WYE BRIDGE

MONSAL DALE: WATER WHEEL

WINSTER AND BONSALL MOOR—11 MILES

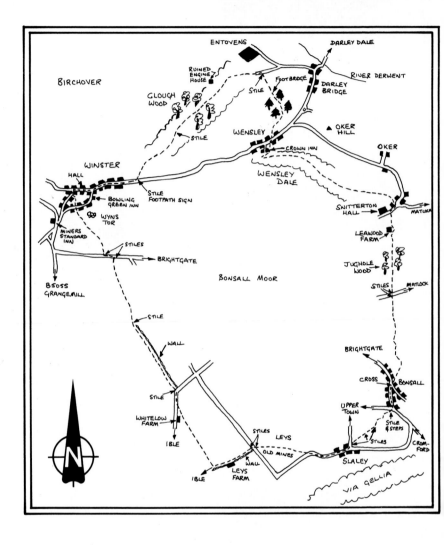

WINSTER—Former lead-mining village. Main street is mostly 18th Century, complete with Hall and Market Hall—now National Trust.

SNITTERTON—The Hall is believed to have been built by John Milward in 1631. The bull-ring is one of only a handful left in the Peak District, and was formerly a popular feature at markets and fairs.

BONSALL—Lead-mining village with many shafts in the surrounding area. The Cross with its thirteen steps is unique in Derbyshire, and on Market days butter and eggs were sold from them. The King's Head Inn dates back to the 16th Century.

WALK NO 9—
WINSTER AND BONSALL MOOR—
11 Miles—allow 5 hours

BASIC ROUTE— *Winster—Clough Wood—Wensley—Wensley Dale—Snitterton—Jughole Wood—Bonsall—Slaley—Leys Farm—Winster Moor, Wyns Tor—Winster.*

MAP— *1:25,000 O.S. Outdoor Leisure Map—The White Peak.*

CAR PARK— *Central Winster—no official car park.*

ABOUT THE WALK— A walk in limestone country close to the edge of the National Park. Many of the paths are little used, but provide stunning views over Matlock and southern Peakland. Several interesting villages are passed, including Bonsall's historic Cross and Snitterton's 17th Century Hall and ancient bull-ring.

WALKING INSTRUCTIONS— Walk along the Main Street of Winster, towards Matlock. En route you pass the Market House on your right and Leacroft Garage on your left. Almost ½ mile from the Market Place you pass a ruined barn on your left. Shortly afterwards on your right is the School sign, and on your left is the stile and path for Clough Wood. Leave the road here and descend the fields to your right, via the stiles. After ½ mile cross the small stream and follow the distinct path along the edge of the wood. During the summer months this path becomes overgrown but is quite passable. ½ mile along here you reach a wide ascending track and a footpath sign. Ascend the track with the remains of an old lead-mining engine house on your left. ¼ mile later turn right along the minor road beside the wood. Just after ¼ mile you reach double metal gates on your left, across a factory road. Turn right here through a wooden stile and cross the field to the trees. Here you find a definite path as you descend through the pine trees to a footbridge. Beyond you ascend gradually, even using some stone steps. At the twin stiles a little later the path divides. Turn right and follow the ascending path across two well-stiled fields to a walled grass track. Turn left and walk along this and along a house drive—Homelea—to the stile and road in Wensley. The footpath sign here states the path is for Stanton Moor and Birchover. Cross the road and, as signposted, follow the tarmaced path to your right, for Matlock. This brings you out just below the Crown Inn. Turn left and follow the descending track to your right into Wensley Dale. Turn left at the dale bottom and walk along the dale floor, crossing two stiles before turning right as marked in bold letters on a barn—'Footpath to Matlock'. Keep the wall on your left before passing through a stile and crossing the fields to the immediate left of Snitterton. At the triple footpath sign turn right into Snitterton.

Turn right along the farm road and take the first road on your left for Leawood Farm. Go through the gate on the left of the farm before curving right along the track. After 50 feet turn left and ascend direct, still on a track, past a water trough. At the very top of the field go through the gate and continue ascending steeply through Jughole Wood. At the top you pass a deep limestone 'hole' on your left. Ascend the stile and cross a field to a minor road from Matlock and footpath sign—Snitterton. Cross the road to the next stile and cross the subsequent field to a stile and onto a walled track. Turn left and follow this as it descends; taking the walled path on your left after ¼ mile. This soon becomes a concrete path as you descend into Bonsall at the historic Market Cross. Walk past the King's Head Inn and descend 'Yeoman Street'. At the next cross turn right and left immediately up the ascending stone- stepped path. Follow the stiles as you cross the fields to the road on the outskirts of Slaley.

BONSALL CROSS

Turn left and walk through the hamlet, bearing right and passing a telephone kiosk on your left. ¼ mile later, on the second curve, leave the road on your right beside the gateposts and cross to a stone stile. The pathline is faint, but the many stiles guide you across the fields to a minor road ½ mile away. Cross this and walk beside the wall on your left to Leys Farm. In the second field from the farm, notice the stile on your left; here you turn right and head directly for Winster 3 miles away. The path is very well-stiled, and after ½ mile, just beyond Whitelow Farm, you walk along a track—'Unsuitable for Motors' for 100 yards to the first corner. Here turn left and keep the wall on your right as you cross further fields. After almost 1 mile pass through a stile on your right before crossing more fields to the minor Bonsall Road, ½ mile away. Turn left, and two fields on your right is the stile and path for Winster. Ascend the field to a stile before bearing left as you descend the fields past Wyns Tor Rocks to the southern edge of the village. Turn right and left almost immediately down a tarmaced path, which will lead you down to West Bank and Winster's Main Street.

WINSTER MORRIS DANCERS c. 1952

PAINTING OF WINSTER CHURCH – 1870

WINSTER MARKET HOUSE – c. 1900

31

SOUTH OF MATLOCK—16 MILES

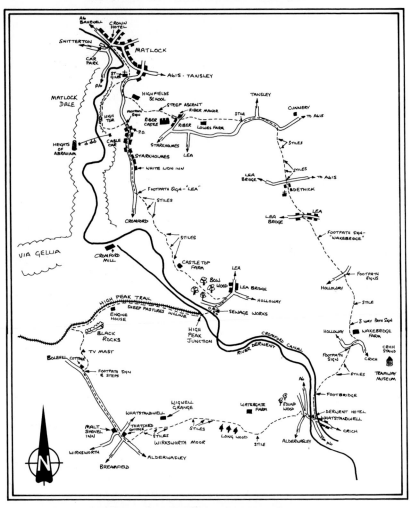

HIGH PEAK TRAIL SIGN

WALK NO 10—SOUTH OF MATLOCK—
16 Miles—allow 7 hours

BASIC ROUTE—*Matlock—Riber—Dethick—Lea—Wakebridge—Cromford Canal—Whatstandwell—Long Wood—Park Wood—Wirksworth Moor—Black Rocks—High Peak Trail—Bow Wood—Starkholmes—High Tor—Matlock Bridge.*

MAP—*1:25,000 O.S. Outdoor Leisure Map—The White Peak.*

CAR PARK—*Beside Matlock Bridge and Railway Station.*

ABOUT THE WALK—To the south of Matlock and outside the National Park is a surprisingly good walking area. In this very diverse walk you will see historical buildings, examples of industrial archaeology, tourist attractions and extensive views whilst walking in both limestone and gritstone countryside.

WALKING INSTRUCTIONS—From the car park entrance on the A6 road, opposite the Midland Bank, turn left over the bridge and turn right and walk beside the Gardens and recreation area. Continue past the boating lake and onto the small road. At the end of this turn right and ascend the cobbled path to the road—Church Street—with St. Giles Church on your right. Turn right, as footpath-signposted—'Path to Riber ¼ mile'. Walk along the road to the entrance of the Charles White School, and on the righthand side of the drive is the signposted and fenced path for Riber. Follow this tarmaced and later cobbled path beside the school and up the hillside to the immediate left of Riber Fauna Reserve. Descend the road, and at the road junction 120 yards later turn right then left, as footpath-signposted, and cross the field to a stile. Turn right and walk along the track to Lowes Farm. Keep straight ahead to the next stile and onto the subsequent ones. After ½ mile you reach a minor road with the stile tucked in a corner on your right. Turn left and walk along the road, keeping straight ahead at the T-junction ¼ mile later. Just after a further ¼ mile the minor road turns sharp left at a small wood. Turn right onto a walled path. After a few yards turn left through a stile and walk round the edge of the field to your right—as arrowed in yellow. Ascend a stile and keep the wall/field boundary on your right as you descend the fields to the road junction in front of Dethick village. Cross the road and walk into the hamlet. In front of Badminton Farm gates, turn right along the walled path to Dethick Church. Go through the gate and cross the field to Swinepark Wood. Don't go through the first stile into the wood, but walk along the wood perimeter to the next stile; then enter the wood and follow the path, across a footbridge and up to the road in Lea village.

CROWN SQUARE, MATLOCK

33

Turn right then left past a chapel and track to a stile. Cross the field to another stile in the top lefthand corner. Cross another stile and field to a small ditch. As footpath—signposted—'Wakebridge'—leave the ditch to a stile and cross the next few fields, all well-stiled, and in ½ mile reach a minor road. Cross this as footpath-signposted; first on a track then path to another track. Turn right along the walled track, keeping a wood on your immediate left. After ¼ mile turn left, passing a triple footpath sign on your right. Walk past the righthand side of Wakebridge Farm to a stile and road. Turn right, and 75 yards later, at another footpath sign, turn left and descend the field gently at first to a gate gap. Then descend more steeply to a stone stile and into a wood. Turn right along the wide path and follow it as it passes several impressive gritstone quarries on your left. After ¼ mile cross a minor road and descend to a footbridge over the Cromford Canal. Turn right and right again onto the towpath and walk beside the canal for ¼ mile. At the road turn right and descend to the A6 road and the Derwent Hotel. Cross the bridge over the River Derwent and take the second road on your left—New Road. After 30 yards turn right through a stile along a signposted path. After 50 yards the path swings left to a private drive. Cross this and, as signposted, follow the path on the left of the drive. Keep to the left of the house as you pass through a stile and ascend the field to another stile. Keep the field boundary on your left, and after the third stile turn right along a faint path towards the top of a small wood on your right. At the corner of the wall is a stile. Walk through the wood to a wooden stile, and for the next four fields keep the perimeter wall of Long Wood on your left. In the fourth field leave the woodside and cross the well-stiled fields. At the end of the third you reach a stile, small stream and track through a wood. Turn left along this to another stile. Cross the next field to a stile beside a tree trunk; far on your right is Wigwell Grange. Continue ahead to another stile and walled track. Upon reaching the road, turn right to the road junction close to the Malt Shovel Inn. Walk past the righthand side of the inn on the Bolehill/Cromford road. Keep to this road for ¾ mile, passing Spitewinter House on your left. Where the road descends and turns left, on your right and close to a cottage is the path sign and stile. Turn right and ascend the steps onto the hillside. Turn left and follow the well-worn path to a triangulation pillar and TV mast on your right. Keep to this path and follow it to the Black Rocks and High Peak Trail.

Turn right and walk along the trail for the next 1½ miles to its end at the Cromford Canal. Cross the canal and walk along the path inbetween the sewage works. At the road turn right, and ¼ mile later, just before John Smedley Works, leave the road via a stile and walk through Bow Wood. After ½ mile reach a track then tarmaced lane. Turn left along this, and, just past the wood on your right, leave it at a wooden stile. Ascend slightly to a stone stile, and follow a grass path past a well to another wooden stile at the entrance to another wood. Follow the path through the wood to a stile and cross the next field to a track. Turn left along this for 40 yards, before turning right over a wooden stile and ascending the field, passing through a solitary stile. At the next stile you enter woodland again before walking round the right of a house to path sign—'Lea'—and the Starkholmes road. Turn right and walk along this for ¾ mile, passing the White Lion Inn on your right. Just after the Post Office turn left along the road between the houses—also footpath-signed—'Matlock Bath' —and enter the grounds of High Tor; a small admission charge here. Ascend through the ground to the Summit Cafe. Descend the track—signposted 'Matlock'. At the other entrance to the grounds turn left and descend to the Derwent River. Don't cross it, but turn right along the path, which will return you to the recreation area and boating lake that you walked past at the beginning. Turn left, and walk past this back to Crown Square and the Railway Station.

DETHICK CHURCH

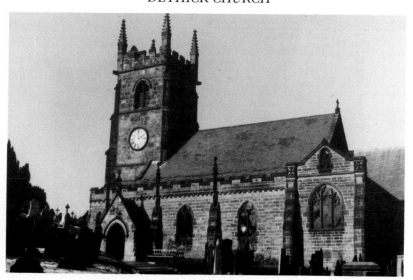

ST. GILES CHURCH, MATLOCK

RIVER DANE—12 MILES

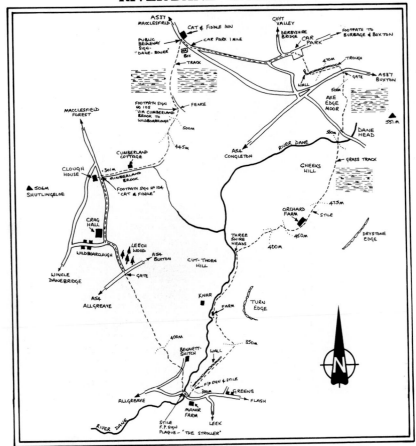

TYPICAL PEAK DISTRICT STILE

THREE SHIRE HEADS—Where the counties of Staffordshire, Cheshire and Derbyshire meet. The bridges are the remains of the important packhorse routes that crossed this area. One of the pools here is aptly named—'Panniers Pool'.

WALK NO 11—RIVER DANE—
12 Miles—allow 5 hours

BASIC ROUTE—*Derbyshire Bridge Car Park—Axe Edge Moor—Dane Head—Orchard Common—Three Shire Heads—River Dane—Manor Farm—Leech Wood—Crag Hall—Cumberland Brook—Cat & Fiddle Inn—Derbyshire Bridge Car Park.*

MAP—*1:25,000 O.S. Outdoor Leisure Map—The White Peak.*

CAR PARK—*Derbyshire Bridge. Grid Ref. SK019716.*

ABOUT THE WALK—Much of the route lies across bleak moorland following little used paths. The views are extensive, and the River Dane and Three Shire Heads are two exceptionally attractive places. The final section up Cumberland Brook to the Cat & Fiddle Inn is rewarding walking, leaving a mile of descent back to the start.

WALKING INSTRUCTIONS—From the toilet block in the car park, turn right and ascend the signposted track—'Berry Clough'—above the car park. After 120 yards turn right off the track at the start of a stone wall on your right. The pathline is faint, but cross the grassy surface to a wall on your right ¼ mile away. Keep the wall on your immediate right to a walled grass track 200 yards away. Turn left and follow this track, with the wall on your left, for the next ½ mile. As you near the main road—A54—you pass a small water trough on your left. Turn right to the road, cross it, and go through the wooden gate on your left onto another track. This will lead you across Axe Edge Moor. After ¼ mile you reach a circular ruined shaft on your right. Turn left here, following a path, and after 150 yards you reach another track. Turn right along this and follow it to the minor road at Dane Head, ½ mile away, where there is a footpath sign—'Goyt Valley'.

Turn right along the road, and after 50 yards left onto a grass track, which you can see ascending the moorland beyond. Cross the infant River Dane, and ¼ mile later cross two stiles at a wall and continue on a track. ¼ mile later, and just after a NCB shaft cone, you join another track coming in from your left. Bear right along the track. After 200 yards, and just past a small quarry on your right, leave the track and head for Orchard Farm. Ascend the stile and walk past the buildings, keeping them on your right. After the last wall you follow a track to a small cottage. Here turn left and descend the field to a wooden stile. Turn right and follow the track with the small stream on your left for the next ½ mile to Three Shire Heads. Just before the packhorse bridge, turn left on the well-trodden track. Cross another packhorse bridge, and after 150 yards take the right track above the River Dane. ½ mile later take the right track, but do not cross the river, to a small farm. Go through the gate and ascend the subsequent field to a wooden stile. Turn right along the field edge to a stone stile. At the end of the wall on your left, bear left to a track. Turn right and follow the grass track, not the gravel track. Go through the gate, and where the wall on your left turns sharp left, turn right and cross the field to a stile. You are now on easier terrain as you descend the next few fields, keeping the wall on your immediate right. It is all well-stiled. After the fourth field you pass a footpath sign before reaching the minor road above Manor Farm.

Turn right along the road to the Gradbach Methodist Chapel, dated 1849. On the other side of Dane Cottage, ascend the stone steps and follow the ascending signposted footpath. On the left of the steps is a small plaque to Clifford Rathbone 1907-1975—a local historian known as 'The Stroller'. At the top of the path turn right on a minor road near Bennettshitch. Immediately leave the road via a gate on your left and follow

the walled track to a farm building. Go through the gate to the wall and ascend the field to its top righthand corner. Keep a small stream on your left to gain a stone ladder stile. The pathline is faint; pass through a gap in the next stone wall and keep the fence on your immediate right. Go through a gate and ascend onto the high ground and follow this level to a gate in the next wall. Just beyond is a very small quarry and a well-defined path, which you follow down the grassy moorland to the Wildboarclough 'T' junction with the A54 road, a little over ¼ mile away.

Descend the road towards Wildboarclough, with Leech Wood on your right. Almost ½ mile later, turn right in front of Crag Hall and follow this road for a little over ½ mile. Just before Clough House turn right onto the signposted track—sign No. 104 'Cat & Fiddle'. After 150 yards cross a footbridge on your left and continue on the track, with the trees and Cumberland Brook on your immediate right. ½ mile from the bridge, pass through a gate and continue ahead on a track with the infant brook as your companion. You begin climbing in earnest up Danethorn Hollow into moorland country. After ¼ mile you reach a wall on your left; keep to the well-used path on the right of it as you ascend more gently to the path from Danebower Hollow, ¼ mile away. At the fence is sign No. 105—'Via Cumberland Brook to Wildboarclough'. Turn left onto a well-travelled path and track, and follow this now level passage to the Cat & Fiddle Inn, ¾ mile away. Turn right at the inn along the A537 road. Opposite the AA box on your right is the No Through Road to the car park. Turn left and follow this descending road back to your starting point.

CAT & FIDDLE INN

THREE SHIRE HEADS

FORMER POST OFFICE, WILDBOARCLOUGH

REEF KNOLLS—13 MILES

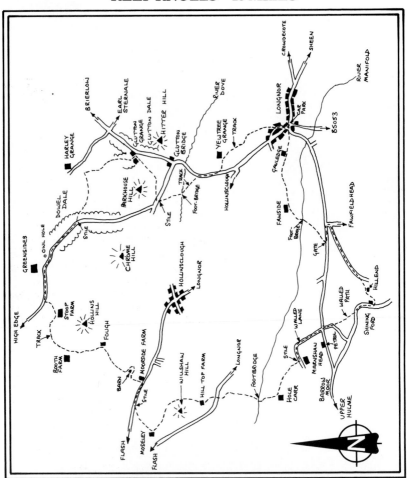

LONGNOR MARKET TOLLS

WALK NO 12—REEF KNOLLS—
13 *Miles—Allow 5/6 hours*

BASIC ROUTE—*Longnor—Yewtree Grange—Glutton Grange—Dowel Dale—Owl Hole—Stoop Farm—Booth Farm—Fough—Moorside—Hill Top Farm—Hole Carr—Shining Ford—The Hills—Fawside—Longnor.*

MAP—*1:25,000 O.S. Outdoor Leisure Map—The White Peak.*

CAR PARK—*Longnor Market Place.*

ABOUT THE WALK—A very rewarding walk along little-used paths. First walking through limestone country and past the reef knolls of Parkhouse Hill, Hitter Hill and Chrome Hill close to the Derbyshire/Staffordshire boundary. The second half over gritstone edges and pleasant farming countryside. Distance and dramatic views are the walk's keynote.

WALKING INSTRUCTIONS—From Longnor Market Place, walk past the Horse Shoe Inn onto the Buxton Road. 50 yards along here, at the start of Church Street, just after passing a chapel on your right, walk up the small road between the houses. Just round the first bend on your right will be found an upright footpath sign. Turn right and follow this path to a stile, and along the lawn edge of the house on your right to the small stile gate. Keep the wall on your right as you cross the next field to two stiles. Over these and the view unfolds. Descend to your left down a grass path to the track on the left of Underhill Farm. Turn left and walk along the track to a small cottage. Turn right over a stile on the immediate right of the building. Descend the next field with the hedge on your right. Just past a farm on your right you reach a tarmaced track. Turn left and ascend this past Yewtree Grange to the Buxton Road (B5053). Turn right, and after 100 yards turn left along another tarmaced track. Where the track turns right to the last house on your right, keep straight ahead to the wooden stile. Cross another stile and bear right, descending to the hawthorn trees and down to the River Dove and footbridge. Pass the stone wall on your right before gaining the stile ahead. Cross the tarmaced road and across the open field beneath Parkhouse Hill to a white painted stone stile. Cross the next field to a gate, and the next to the righthand side of Glutton Grange. Go through three gates to the farm track in front of the house. Turn left along the track, and just after a gate go through another on your right and walk along the track with the wall on your immediate left. Walk up the shallow dale for the next half mile with the wall on your left. Ascend a stone stile at the top onto a track. Turn left along this, and after the first gate turn right through a stile and cross a large field with the wall well to your right. After ¼ mile ascend a stone stile, near the corner of the field, and descend abruptly to the minor road through Dowel Dale.

Ascend the road for ½ mile to the limestone—Owl Hole—on your right. Continue on the road to a gate and bear left at the entrance to Greensides Farm. Go through another gate, and 150 yards later, where the track bears right at a yellow gritting box, turn left on the track to Stoop Farm. Where it descends to your left, leave the track and bear towards the righthand side of the trees and walk between the widely-spaced walls above the farm. After 150 yards you reach another track, which you follow to the entrance of Booth Farm ¼ mile away. Continue on the track—not to the farm—and in ¼ mile reach Fough. Turn right in front of the house to a gate. Turn left to another gate before turning right and descending first to a stile (one upright only) before reaching the footbridge over a brook. Ascend the field beyond, keeping the gritstone wall on your left. At the end of the field turn left to the barn and ascend the curving track to the top of Moor Side. At the top of the edge keep the wall on your left to a gate on the right of Moorside Farm. Walk along the farm drive to the road. Turn right and descend the road. 200 yards later, in the bottom of the descent, turn left over a stile on the righthand side of the gate, just before a building. Ascend the field, following a shallow ditch on your left. At the top and in front of the house— Moseley—is a stile. Don't go over this, but turn left to another stile and curve round the next field to a brook and bridge and ascend the track here to your left, then right to Willshaw Farm. Walk through the farmyard to a stile. Keep the wall on your left as you contour round to a gap in the next wall. Maintain your height as you curve round to another wall, which you keep on your immediate right. Cross a small ditch and walk through Hill Top Farm. Continue ahead on a faint track, and after the first field turn right to a gate and road.

Cross the road to another gate and descend a sunken track. After 150 yards turn right and descend steeply to a wall full of gaps and descend the next two fields, keeping the wall on your left. At the end of the second field, cross two foot-bridges before walking up the lefthand side of the field to the farm - Hole Carr. At the buildings turn right and then left onto the farm track and walk past the house. Go through a gate, and at the end of the field you will find a white painted stile. Pass through this before ascending to another stile. Pass through a wooden stile before reaching a gate and tarmaced road beyond. Turn left and follow this road for the next ½ mile. Upon reaching the Longnor road, cross it and follow the road opposite. At the first corner, keep straight ahead on a walled path. ¼ mile later join a road and turn left. After crossing Shining Ford, go through the green gate on your left. At the next gate bear right around the wall before turning left for Hillend. Walk in front of the house on the track up to the tarmaced road. Turn left and follow this for ½ mile. Turn left and left again and, 150 yards later, turn right through the gate and cross the field to a footbridge before ascending to Fawside Farm. Walk through the farm and, where the track bears left, keep straight ahead to stiles, footbridge and more stiles to Gauledge. Walk along the track back into central Longnor.

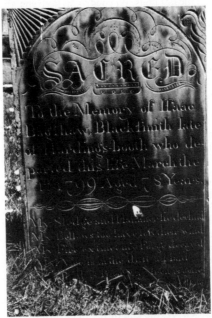

BLACKSMITHS TOMB – LONGNOR CHURCHYARD

GRASS OF PARNASSUS

WALKING IN THE MANIFOLD VALLEY

THE HILL AND RIVER HAMPS—12 MILES

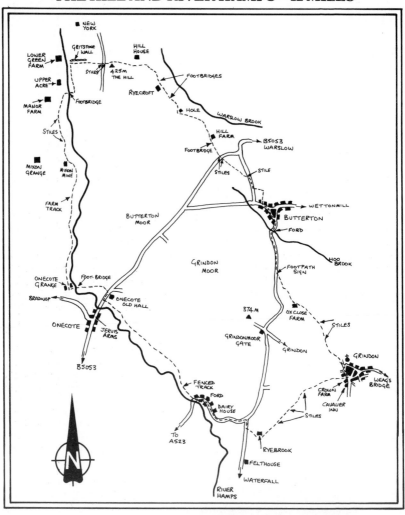

BLACK LION INN, BUTTERTON

WALK NO 13—THE HILL & RIVER HAMPS
12 Miles—allow 5 hours

BASIC ROUTE—*Grindon—Ryebrook—Ford—Onecote—Onecote Grange—Mixon Mine—River Hamps—Lower Green Farm—The Hill (Trig 425 metres)—Hole—Butterton—Oxclose Farm—Grindon.*

MAP—*1:25,000 O.S. Outdoor Leisure Map—The White Peak.*

CAR PARK—*No official car park.*

ABOUT THE WALK—Surprisingly, this area of the National Park is overlooked and rarely walked. I first walked this in 1968 and saw no other walker; fifteen years later I again saw no one! The paths are little used but well-stiled, and pass through delightful countryside. The view from 'The Hill' is extensive and well worth the walk to sample. Four quiet attractive villages are passed through en route.

WALKING INSTRUCTIONS—Starting from the church in Grindon, turn left along the road away from the church, towards the Cavalier Inn. Turn right before it on the open road, and on the immediate right of Crown Farm on your left is the stone stile. Several more wooden stiles lead you across the fields for the next mile to Ryebrook Farm. Walk around the farm to your right to a stone stile and farm track. Cross this and ascend the field to another stone stile and minor road. Turn right then left, and descend the road to the hamlet—Ford, ½ mile away. Don't cross the River Hamps at the bridge, but keep ahead and walk round through the farm to your right. Just past the house go through a gate and walk along a fenced track. Cross a stile, then another, keeping the fence then wall on your right. At the cattle grid and track to Bullcough, keep straight ahead over the stile. The pathline is now non-existent, but simply cross the field keeping the beech trees on your left. Just beyond, descend to the valley floor and ¼ mile later just above the river is a stone stile. Descend the field to another stile and the road, with Onecote village and Jervis Arms on your left.

Turn right, and 50 yards later opposite the entrance to Onecote Old Hall is the stone stile, on your left. Ascend the short field to two stone stiles, with a house and garden on your left. Just beyond the stone wall turn left through a gap to another stone stile. In the next field cross a farm track before reaching a footbridge. Cross this and walk up the field on the immediate left of Onecote Grange.

At the metal gate on your right, go through this and through the farmyard and keep on the farm track. After the first stile bear right on the track, with the infant River Hamps below on your right. Follow the track for the next 1¼ miles. After one mile keep to the righthand track to reach Mixon Mine House. The path goes up the drive and past the house, where there is a white-painted stone stile. Cross the next fields via the stiles, and after ½ mile, at the track from Manor Farm, turn right and descend to the infant river, which is crossed via a footbridge. Turn left and, although there is no defined path, it is well-stiled as you keep to the righthand side of the river valley. After ¼ mile you reach a wall, footbridge and track in front of Lower Green Farm. Turn right and keep the wall on your left as you ascend first to a stone stile then another just before a minor road. Cross this to a wooden stile and the triangulation pillar on 'The Hill'—425 metres. The view is extensive. Descend steeply to the wooden stile on the right of Hill House. Continue descending to a stone stile and track. Turn right into the farm, and left almost immediately over a stile in between the farm engines. Descend the field passing a water trough, keeping the wall on your immediate left. At the end of the field turn right, keeping the fence on your left to a footbridge. Cross this, and ascend first to two gates then another footbridge. At the end of the second field go through another gate and curve to your right on a track to Hole Farm. Turn left and walk in front of the farm on the track. 100 yards later, where it turns left and descends to Warslow Brook, keep straight ahead—no pathline—but after 75 yards you reach a stone stile. Beyond you reach a track, which you follow to Hill Farm, the last part being a walled path. Walk through the farm on your right, and where the track curves right keep straight ahead to a wooden stile and footbridge. Ascend the field beyond to a wooden stile and minor road. Cross this to the stone stile and cross the next two fields, with the stone wall on your right. At the end of the next field ascend a wooden stile, then another to the minor road. Turn right, and 50 yards later left over the stone stile. At the end of the second field, go through the stile and turn right and enter Butterton village via Croft Head Farm.

Turn left and 50 yards later turn right—'Grindon 2 miles'—and descend to the ford over Hoo Brook. Keep on the road, and ascend for another ¼ mile to a footpath sign on your left. Go through the stile and keep to the righthand edge of the field to a stone stile. Keep the field boundary on your immediate right to two more stiles and a gate before Oxclose Farm. Continue ahead to a stile, then keep the fence on your right to a limestone stile. Again keep the field boundary on your right for the final ½ mile. After the final stile the minor road in front of Grindon Church is reached. Turn right, and after a few yards the church is on your left and your starting point.

GRINDON CHURCH

RAVENS TOR, MILLER'S DALE

THE ROACHES AND TITTESWORTH RESERVOIR—
13 MILES

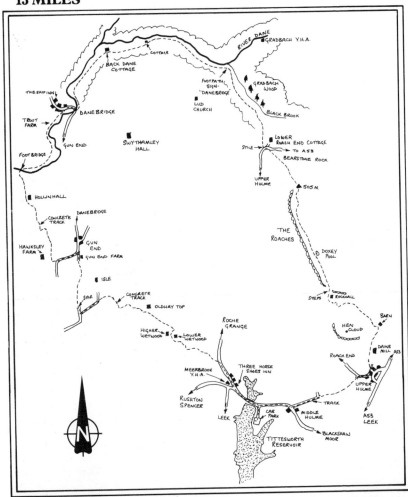

GRADBACH YOUTH HOSTEL

WALK NO 14—
THE ROACHES & TITTESWORTH RESERVOIR
13 Miles—allow 5 hours

BASIC ROUTE— *Tittesworth Reservoir—Upper Hulme—Well Farm—*
The Roaches—Trig Point 505 metres—Black Brook—River Dane—Danebridge—
River Dane—Gun End House—Lower Wetwood—Meerbrook—Tittesworth
Reservoir.

MAP— *1:25,000 O.S. Outdoor Leisure Map—The White Peak.*

CAR PARK— *Tittesworth Reservoir—Amenity area.*

ABOUT THE WALK— A magnificent walk across the gritstone moorland and crag—The Roaches. Followed by a delightful wooded walk along the River Dane before crossing the fields to Meerbrook and reservoir. An exceptional walk.

WALKING INSTRUCTIONS— From the car park entrance, turn right and walk along the minor road for just over ¼ mile to Middle Hulme Farm. Turn left and walk along the track, and after ¼ mile, where the track turns sharp left, keep straight ahead over the wooden stile. Cross the field to a railed path across a ditch, before turning right and keeping the ditch on your right for the next ¼ mile to a farm. Walk through the farmyard and bear left up the farm track to the road in Upper Hulme. Turn right and descend the road to the works complex and Roaches Craft Centre. Where the road turns sharp right at the stream, keep straight ahead and ascend the concrete drive on the left of Carriage House. Pass through a gate before descending a track to the stream in front of Dains Mill. Keep the stream on your right as you follow a small path leading to several stiles. After 200 yards you approach a small stone barn. Turn left here—a path is discernible—to a stone stile and track. Turn left and follow the white chipped track, ignoring the tracks that branch to your left and right. Follow the track for ¼ mile to the entrance of Well Farm. Turn left over a stile and walk round the lefthand side of the farm to another stile and plaque - Roaches Estate. Cross the next field on a distinct path to a stile and grass track. Turn left, and a few yards later right, and ascend the path between the rock outcrops to the main buttress of The Roaches. Keep to the path beneath the rocks for ¼ mile before turning right up a track to the crest of the rocks and moorland. Turn left and walk along the top of The Roaches for the next 1 ½ miles. First passing Doxey Pool on your right and, almost a mile later, the triangulation pillar - 505 metres. ½ mile descent from here brings you to the minor road, close to Roach End.

Cross the road to your right and walk down the start of the track for Lower Roach End Cottage. After 50 yards turn left to a stone stile. Pass through it and turn right, keeping the wall on your right. The path is well-defined. After 200 yards you pass a footpath sign, and shortly afterwards ascend slightly into beech trees. Continue descending, now in pine trees, keeping to the righthand path at the first path junction and the lefthand path at the second junction. All the time you keep high above Black Brook. Just after ½ mile from the beech trees you reach the brook at a ford. Keep the brook on your right to a footbridge and path sign—'Roach End & Danebridge'. Turn left then right and keep on the well-trodden path to Danebridge 2 ½ miles away. After almost 1 mile you leave the River Dane and ascend to a small farm, which you walk past on its lefthand side via two stiles. Pass Back Dane Cottage ½ mile later, and continue on the path—sometimes a track—and pass through woodland to reach the bridge over the Dane, ½ mile away. Turn right and follow the road over the bridge. 100 yards later turn left at the telephone kiosk and walk along the track to Tolls Farm. 30 yards later ascend the stile on your left and follow the 'concessionary path to Gighall and Rushton'. Cross the field and walk along the track through a trout farm. At the cottage, bear left over the two stiles and continue walking beside the River Dane. 250 yards later keep the wood wall on your right for the next ¼ mile before crossing a wooden stile and returning to the riverside. ¼ mile later cross the river via a metal footbridge.

On the lefthand side of the house is the stile. Ascend the field beyond and, after the initial ascent, turn right to a stile beside an oak tree. Cross the next field, aiming for the farm buildings—Hollin Hall. Walk through the farm onto the track on your left. At first this is a walled track, but soon becomes a concrete track which you follow for ¾ mile. At the T- junction on the left of Hawksley Farm, turn left to the minor road opposite a metal path sign—'Gighall 1 mile via Dane Valley'. Turn left along the road to Gun End House. Turn right here up the track past Gun End Farm on your left. Keep on the track to a gate and then along a grass track with a small wood on your right. ¼ mile from the trees cross a stile and reach a tarmaced lane. Turn left along this, and after ¼ mile continue ahead on a 'Private Road'. This soon becomes another concrete farm road, which you follow for ½ mile to the sharp lefthand bend before Oldhay Top. Turn right and descend the field to a stone stile. Ascend this, and descend the next field to your right to another stile, and another wooden stile 75 yards later. Turn right, and walk through Lower Wetwood Farm before turning left onto another concrete farm road. After ¼ mile this becomes a track. Just after a gate, leave the track and pass under the overhead electric cables to a stone stile. Bear left and pass through two field gaps before reaching a wooden gate and the road. Turn right and walk along the road into Meerbrook village. At the road junction, with the YHA on your right and the Three Horse Shoe Inn on your left, turn left along the road, across Tittesworth Reservoir to the car park on your right.

THE ROACHES

50

DANEBRIDGE

THE SHIP INN, DANEBRIDGE

THE RIVER DOVE AND MANIFOLD—24 MILES

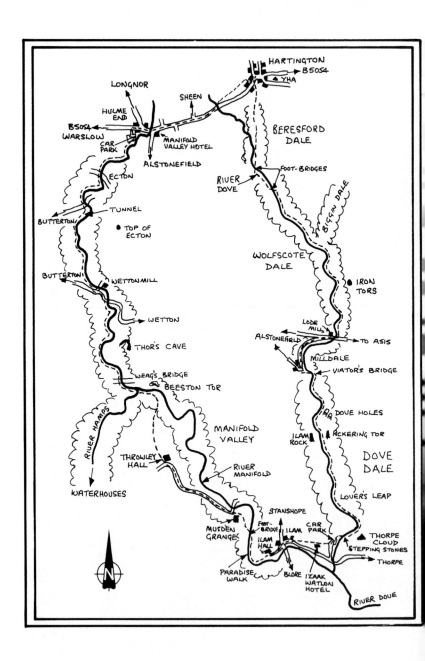

WALK NO 15—
THE RIVER DOVE & MANIFOLD
24 Miles—allow 9/10 hours

BASIC ROUTE—*Hartington—Beresford Dale—Wolfscote Dale—Mill Dale—Dovedale—Ilam—Throwley Hall—Wettonmill—Manifold Valley—Hulme End—Hartington.*

MAP—*1:25,000 O.S. Outdoor Leisure Map—The White Peak.*

CAR PARK—*Hartington.*

ABOUT THE WALK—Although long, this walk has few equals for the scenery to be passed. It is a challenge to walk it in a day, but it also makes a good weekend trip, with Ilam as the halfway point. The route follows well-used paths and is very straightforward to follow. It still remains one of my most enjoyable long walks in the Peak District.

REFRESHMENT POINTS & ACCOMMODATION—
Milldale; Ilam; Wettonmill and Hulme End.

WALKING INSTRUCTIONS—The walk begins just past the Charles Cotton Hotel in Hartington. The path sign is on your left beside the public toilets. The path takes you first into Beresford Dale before crossing the River Dove and walking down Wolfscote Dale to Lode Bridge. Here a short road walk down to Milldale village brings you to Viators Bridge and the path down Dove Dale. Cross the stepping stones and walk down the tarmaced road to the carpark on your left. Here turn right and cross the fields, close to the Izaak Walton Hotel, to Ilam village.

Walk past the church to Ilam Hall—National Trust Information Office and Youth Hostel. Reach the Manifold River and walk beside it to a footbridge. Turn left over this and cross the fields on the right of Musden Grange. Just beyond, gain the single track road and follow this to Throwley Hall. Turn left in the farmyard and follow the path over the field to a small strip wood. Ascend the stiles and descend to the Manifold at Beeston Tor. You now follow the line of the Manifold & Leek Railway, which ceased in 1934. The surface is now tarmaced, and along this you walk past Thor's Cave to Wettonmill, through a tunnel 1½ miles later, past Ecton to Hulme End. A short road walk from here—2 miles—returns you to Hartington. At Hartington Bridge, just on the Derbyshire boundary, you can follow the path across the fields to Hartington.

DOVEDALE, STEPPING STONES
53

OTHER BOOKS BY JOHN N.MERRILL
& PUBLISHED BY JNM PUBLICATIONS

DAY WALK GUIDES

PEAK DISTRICT: SHORT CIRCULAR WALKS Fifteen carefully selected walks—3 to 5 miles—starting from a car park. The walks cover the variety of the area—the gritstone edges, limestone dales, and peat moorland. All follow well defined paths; include a pub for lunch; and are suitable for all the family. 44 pages 16 maps 32 photographs **ISBN 0 907496 16 4**

PEAK DISTRICT TOWN WALKS Twelve short circular walks around the principal towns and villages of the Peak District. Including Castleton, Buxton, Hathersage, Eyam,Tissington and Ashbourne. Each walk has a detailed map and extensive historical notes complete with pictures. 60 pages 12 maps 96 photographs **ISBN 0 907496 20 2**

PEAK DISTRICT: LONG CIRCULAR WALKS Fifteen differing walks 12 to 18 miles long for the serious hiker. Many follow lesser used paths in the popular areas, giving a different perspective to familiar landmarks. 64 pages 16 maps 28 photographs **ISBN 0 907496 17 2**

WESTERN PEAKLAND—CIRCULAR WALKS The first book to cover this remarkably attractive side of the National Park—west of Buxton. The guide combines both long and short walks. 25 -3 to 11 mile long walks with extremely detailed maps to help you explore the area. 48 pages 23 maps 22 photographs **ISBN 0 907496 15 6**

12 SHORT CIRCULAR WALKS AROUND MATLOCK 12 walks of about 4 miles long into the Matlock area rich in history and folklore and make ideal family outings. Included is an 'alpine' walk, using Matlock Bath's cable car as part of the route. 52 pages 44 photographs 12 maps **ISBN 0 907496 25 3**

SHORT CIRCULAR WALKS IN THE DUKERIES More than 25 walks in the Nottinghamshire/Sherwood Forest area, past many of the historic buildings that make up the Dukeries area. **ISBN 0 907496 29 6**

DERBYSHIRE AND THE PEAK DISTRICT CANAL WALKS More than 20 walks both short and long along the canals in the area—Cromford, Erewash, Chesterfield, Derby, Trent, Peak Forest and Macclesfield canals. **ISBN 0 907496 30 X**

HIKE TO BE FIT: STROLLING WITH JOHN John Merrill's personal guide to walking in the countryside to keep fit and healthy. He describes what equipment to use, where to go, how to map read, use a compass and what to do about blisters. 36 pages 23 photos 2 sketches 3 charts **ISBN 0 907496 19 9**

CHALLENGE WALKS

JOHN MERRILL'S PEAK DISTRICT CHALLENGE WALK A 25 mile circular walk from Bakewell, across valleys and heights involving 3,700 feet of ascent. More than 2,000 people have already completed the walk. A badge and completion certificate is available to those who complete. 32 pages 18 photographs 9 maps
ISBN 0 907496 18 0

JOHN MERRILL'S YORKSHIRE DALES CHALLENGE WALK A 23 mile circular walk from Kettlewell in the heart of the Dales. The route combines mountain, moorlands, limestone country and dale walking with 3,600 feet of ascent. A badge and certificate is available to those who complete the route. 32 pages 16 photographs 8 maps
ISBN 0 907196 28 8

THE RIVER'S WAY A two day walk of 43 miles, down the length of the Peak District National Park. Inaugurated and created by John, the walk starts at Edale, the end of the Pennine Way, and ends at Ilam. Numerous hostels, campgrounds, B&B, and pubs lie on the route, as you follow the five main river systems of the Peak—Noe, Derwent, Wye, Dove, and Manifold. 52 pages 35 photographs 7 maps
ISBN 0 907496 08 3

PEAK DISTRICT: HIGH LEVEL ROUTE A hard 90 mile, weeks walk, around the Peak District, starting from Matlock. As the title implies the walk keeps to high ground while illustrating the dramatic landscape of the Peak District. The walk was inaugurated and created by John and is used by him for training for his major walks! 60 pages 31 photographs 13 maps
ISBN 0 907496 10 5

PEAK DISTRICT MARATHONS The first reference book to gather together all the major and classical long walks of the Peak District between 25 and 50 miles long. Many are challenge walks with badges and completion cards for those who complete. The longest walk—280 miles —inaugurated by John is around the entire Derbyshire boundary. Each walk has a general map, accommodation list, and details of what guides and maps are needed. 56 pages 20 photographs 20 maps
ISBN 0 907496 13 X

HISTORICAL GUIDES

WINSTER—A VISITOR'S GUIDE A detailed look at a former lead mining community which still retains a Morris dancing team and annual pancake races. A two mile walk brings you to many historical buildings including the 17th century Market House. Illustrated by old photographs. 20 pages 21 photographs 1 map
ISBN 0 907496 21 0

DERBYSHIRE INNS The first book to tell the story behind more than 150 inns in the Peak District and Derbyshire area. With details of legends, murders and historical anecdotes, the book gives added pleasure or impetus to explore the pubs of the region. Profusely illustrated with 65 photographs and a brief history of brewing in Derbyshire. 68 pages 57 photographs 5 maps ISBN 0 907496 11 3

100 HALLS AND CASTLES OF THE PEAK DISTRICT AND DERBYSHIRE A visitor's guide to the principal historical buildings of the region. Many are open to the public and the guide describes the history of the building from the Domesday Book to the present time. The book is illustrated by 120 photographs and makes an excellent souvenir gift of one of England's finest architectural areas. 120 pages 116 photographs 4 maps
ISBN 0 907496 23 7

WALK RECORD CHART

<table>
<tr><td></td><td></td><td>Date
Walked</td></tr>
<tr><td>KINDER'S SOUTHERN EDGE</td><td>10 Miles</td><td></td></tr>
<tr><td>THE PENNINE WAY ALTERNATIVE</td><td>12 Miles</td><td></td></tr>
<tr><td>KINDER DOWNFALL</td><td>12 Miles</td><td></td></tr>
<tr><td>AROUND BLEAKLOW</td><td>20 Miles</td><td></td></tr>
<tr><td>HOPE VALLEY—HIGH LEVEL ROUTE</td><td>13 Miles</td><td></td></tr>
<tr><td>SILLY DALE</td><td>15 Miles</td><td></td></tr>
<tr><td>BAKEWELL AND STANTON MOOR</td><td>15 Miles</td><td></td></tr>
<tr><td>THE MONSAL TRAIL</td><td>18 Miles</td><td></td></tr>
<tr><td>WINSTER AND BONSALL MOOR</td><td>11 Miles</td><td></td></tr>
<tr><td>SOUTH OF MATLOCK</td><td>16 Miles</td><td></td></tr>
<tr><td>RIVER DANE</td><td>12 Miles</td><td></td></tr>
<tr><td>REEF KNOLLS</td><td>13 Miles</td><td></td></tr>
<tr><td>THE HILL AND RIVER HAMPS</td><td>12 Miles</td><td></td></tr>
<tr><td>THE ROACHES
AND TITTESWORTH RESERVOIR</td><td>13 Miles</td><td></td></tr>
<tr><td>THE RIVER DOVE AND MANIFOLD</td><td>24 Miles</td><td></td></tr>
</table>

GET A JOHN MERRILL WALKING BADGE—complete six of these walks and send details and £1.75 payable to JNM Publications.

BEESTON TOR, MANIFOLD VALLEY

56